Flights of Imagination

Flights of Imagination

An Illustrated Anthology of Bird Poetry

Compiled by Mike Mockler

Blandford Press
Poole, Dorset

For Pat

First published in the U.K. 1982 by Blandford Press
Link House, West Street, Poole, Dorset, BH15 1LL

Selection and Arrangement
Copyright © 1982 Blandford Books Ltd.

British Library Cataloguing in Publication Data

Mockler, Michael
    Flights of imagination.
    1. Birds — Poetry   2. English poetry
    I. Title
    821'.008'036   PR1195.B5

Distributed in the United States by
Sterling Publishing Co., Inc.,
2 Park Avenue, New York, N.Y. 10016.

ISBN 0 7137 1164 7

Typeset by Poole Typesetting Co. Ltd.

Printed in Hong Kong by South China Printing Co.

Contents

Foreword

by H.R.H. The Duke of Edinburgh, K.G.,
President of the World Wildlife Fund

If the rate of destruction of the natural environment continues at its present rate for much longer, anyone trying to produce a book like this in future would have to rely on natural history television programs to inspire the poets and stuffed museum specimens to provide the models for the artists.

The World Wildlife Fund exists to finance conservation projects initiated by the International Union for the Conservation of Nature and naturally the bigger the fund the more projects can be undertaken. If W.W.F. fails, such a book will really be a flight of imagination.

BUCKINGHAM PALACE
1982

Introduction

I was like the others, like those who walk along the
seashore in their spring clothes. I used to say like them:
'The sea is green; that white speck up there is a seagull,'
but I didn't feel that it existed, that the seagull was an
'existing seagull' ...

Jean-Paul Sartre

Few people can remain completely unmoved by the sights and sounds of wild birds, with their grace and delicacy of movement, the rich variety of their songs and calls, the subtleties of their colourful plumage and, of course, the marvel of flight. From the enjoyment of the birds themselves it is but a short step to enjoyment of the poetry which captures their beauty and charm in words.

Through the centuries, English writers have found the world of nature, and birds in particular, a source of inspiration, although it was not until the nineteenth century that any English poet attempted to depict the birds in accurate detail as they really are and allowed the birds to be the subject of a poem rather than merely an appendage to it. Not until John Clare, in fact, did any poet write as if the bird 'existed' enabling the reader to feel that the bird was an 'existing bird'.

The tradition of using birds in literature, if not of describing them vividly, can be traced back a long way. In the ninth or tenth century, the unknown author of the Anglo-Saxon poem 'The Seafarer' wrote:

I found my joy in the cry of the gannet
And the call of the curlew rather than in the laughter of men,
In the scream of the gull instead of in the drinking of mead.

By the Middle Ages, some birds had become poetic conventions. In *Troilus and Criseyde*, Chaucer compares his own position as narrator to a helpless lark seized by a sparrowhawk. Then Criseyde, overcoming her fear as she embraces her lover for the first time, is likened to a nightingale which resumes singing after it has been disturbed:

And as the nightingale, when disturbed,
Goes silent, having just begun to sing,
When it hears the herdsman's voice,
Or the sound of someone in the hedgerows moving,
Then afterwards begins again with confident song,
Just so, Criseyde, when her fears had passed,
Opened her heart and revealed to him her true intent.

More than two hundred years later, many of Shakespeare's plays were liberally sprinkled with bird images and allusions. In *Macbeth* alone there are references to crow and rook, owl and raven, kite and falcon, sparrow and wren, eagle and house martin. In most cases, however, the birds are mentioned only in passing, merely serving to form part of the backcloth against which the events of the plays take place. Although Shakespeare was almost certainly familiar with the birds and animals in the hedgerows, fields and woods around Stratford-upon-Avon, where he grew up, they are never allowed to exist in their own right in his plays.

The cuckoo, like the nightingale, has always featured prominently in legend and poetry. Both birds appear in Milton's 'To the Nightingale', written in 1629 when the poet was twenty-one, but only as symbols, nothing more. There is no attempt to depict the birds or their songs, only to make play with the idea that the nightingale is the friend of lovers, the cuckoo the enemy: those lovers who hear the cuckoo sing first in spring will suffer disappointment, while those who hear the nightingale first will have good fortune. The idea is based wholly on a literary tradition dating back at least to the medieval poem 'The Cuckoo and the Nightingale' which was at one time thought to have been written by Chaucer.

Milton's later poetry was a major influence on the style of James Thomson, whose great work, *The Seasons,* was published in its final, complete form in 1746. In it Thomson presents a detailed account of rural life during the different seasons of the year and includes several descriptions of bird behaviour. Some are no more than a continuation of the traditions which had so limited nature poetry for centuries: Philomela, the nightingale, is invoked several times, the lark is 'the messenger of the morn' and birds are given human emotions. Parent birds, for instance, after their young have hatched, are described thus:

> Oh, what passions then,
> What melting sentiments of kindly care,
> On the new parents seize! Away they fly
> Affectionate, and undesiring bear
> The most delicious morsel to their young.

The treatment is too sentimental for twentieth-century tastes but Thomson was evidently writing about events he had actually witnessed in the countryside, a whole range of real birds in real situations, and represents, therefore, a major development:

> The blackbird whistles from the thorny brake,
> The mellow bullfinch answers from the grove;
> Nor are the linnets, o'er the flowering furze
> Poured out profusely, silent...
> ...The jay, the rook, the daw,
> And each harsh pipe, discordant heard alone,
> Aid the full concert; while the stock-dove breathes
> A melancholy murmur through the whole.

He was paving the way for others to follow by showing that poetry could embrace more than just conventional allusions to the traditional birds of poetry which had by this time become lifeless stereotypes, although it must be said that not all who came after followed that lead.

Like Thomson, Wordsworth wrote about the sights and sounds he experienced in the countryside. For him, too, nature was all important. In his old age he recalled how, at the age of fourteen, there came to him a 'consciousness of the infinite variety of natural appearances which had been unnoticed by the poets of any age or country'. He described nature as:

> ...the nurse
> The guide, the guardian of my heart, and soul
> Of all my moral being.

Why then is Wordsworth not represented in this anthology? The answer is simply that for him nature was a personified force, an abstract idea, and not a network of life-forms and occurrences: his major concern was to record the imaginative pleasures, fears and fancies which the countryside can provide, rather than the countryside itself. This is not to say that Wordsworth failed to observe nature closely or even that, on occasions, he did not describe natural events accurately and honestly. In 'The Sparrow's Nest' (1801), he portrays the nest and eggs of a pair of dunnocks.

> Behold, within the leafy shade
> Those bright blue eggs together laid.

and we see from 'A Wren's Nest' (1833) that many features of that bird's nesting habits were known to him. In most cases, though, the birds that Wordsworth describes exist only as far as they affect the poet or those close to him. In 'The Sparrow's Nest', the poet, having briefly depicted the nest and eggs, then concentrates on the reaction of his sister, Dorothy, to the finding of the nest, and his own relationship with her then and in later years. The bird is forgotten. As in 'To the Cuckoo' (1802), 'To a Green Linnet' (1803), and 'To a Skylark' (1805), the bird is no more than a starting point for a train of thought or an outpouring of emotion.

Of course, the two stock birds of poetry have always been the nightingale and the skylark. In *Romeo and Juliet,* Shakespeare was drawing heavily on literary convention when he gave Juliet these lines as she tries to convince Romeo that their wedding night has not yet ended:

> Wilt thougn be gone? it is not yet near day.
> It was the nightingale and not the lark
> That pierc'd the fearful hollow of thine ear.

These two birds prompted what are probably the two most famous English bird poems: Keats' 'Ode to a Nightingale' (1819) and Shelley's 'Ode to a Skylark' (1820). Some readers, picking up this book for the first time, might be surprised to find these two famous poems omitted: a few may be disappointed. Yet a reading of the two poems in question alongside some that have been included will immediately reveal their essential differences and the reason for the deliberate omission. In neither of the two odes is the bird of the title the main subject; nor is it the intention of either poet to present the birds or their behaviour in any detail. The birds are, in fact, a notional presence only, a starting point for the poets' thoughts and fancies and never brought alive as living creatures.

A contemporary of Keats and Shelley was John Clare but, as a nature poet, he has little in common with either of them or with any of his forbears. For Clare was the first English poet to present nature pictorially, lovingly, accurately and knowledgeably. He was the first nature poet in the true sense, being both poet and naturalist, and is, for this reason, the earliest poet whose work appears in this anthology. For him nature was a source of inspiration too but it inspired him to write, not about himself or his feelings, but about what he actually saw and heard in the fields and woods around his Northampton-shire home.

In April 1825, less than six years after Keats had written 'Ode to a Nightingale', Clare wrote the following in his notebook:

I went to take my walk and heard the Nightingale for the first time this season in Royce Wood just at the town end ... we may now be assured that the summer is nigh at hand ... when I was a boy I usd to be very curious to watch the nightingale to find her nest and to observe her color and size for I had heard many odd tales about her and I often observed her habits and found her nest so I shall be able to give you a pretty faithful history – she is a plain bird something like the hedge sparrow in shape and the female Firetail or Redstart in color but more slender than the former and of a redder brown or scorchd color than the latter ... the breast of the male or female is spotted like a young Robin and the feathers on the rump and on parts of the wing are of a fox red or burnt umber hue ... they generally seek the same solitude which they haunted last season and these are the black thorn clumps and thickets about the woods and spinneys.

These are the writings of a dedicated naturalist, a man in love with nature, not the *idea* of nature, a man who possessed the patience, understanding and keen eye that typify the writings of Gilbert White, the great pioneer naturalist who was writing about fifty years earlier. For Clare, each wild bird and creature he watched was interesting in itself, not a mere abstraction, a symbol or a starting point for a train of thought.

Born in 1793, the year that Gilbert White died, Clare has much in common with his predecessor.

Like White, who refused promotion so that he could remain in his beloved Selborne, Clare spent much of his life in one small village, Helpstone, where the constantly-changing local wildlife was a never-ending source of wonder to him.

Clare's conviction that nature in its own right should be regarded as a worthy subject for poetry is obvious:

Pastoral poems are full of nothing but the old threadbare epithets of 'sweet singing cuckoo', 'love lorn nightingale', 'fond turtles', 'sparkling brooks', 'green meadows', 'leafy woods', etc. etc. These make up the creation of Pastoral and descriptive poesy and everything else is reckond low and vulgar. In fact they are too rustic for the fashionable or prevailing system of rhyme till some bold inovating genius rises with a real love for nature and then they will no doubt be considered as great beautys which they really are.

Few would claim that Clare was a 'bold inovating genius' but no one can deny that he possessed a 'real love for nature' or that his nature poems are 'great beautys'. What they may lack in profundity, they make up for in their freshness and honesty.

Look at Clare's 'The Nightingale's Nest' for a perfect example. Even without reference to the detailed field notes quoted above, one would know, immediately upon reading the poem, that the poet is relating a vivid personal experience. He notices tiny details with the eye of both poet and ornithologist:

> dead oaken leaves
> Are placed without and velvet moss within,
> And little scraps of grass, and – scant and spare,
> Of what seem scarce materials – down and hair.

He is the reader's personal guide, pointing out minute details as if a companion on a nature ramble:

> Hark! there she is as usual – let's be hush –
> For in this blackthorn clump, if rightly guessed,
> Her curious house is hidden.

Then, finally, there is the concern for the welfare of the bird, the reaction of the genuine naturalist:

> So even now
> We'll leave it as we found it: safety's guard
> Of pathless solitudes shall keep it still.

It is not surprising that, with the exception of one poem of Alfred Lord Tennyson, John Clare's are the only poems, in this anthology, written before the twentieth century. Nature is so keenly observed and minutely rendered that he would seem to have more in common with poets of this century than his predecessors or contemporaries. So concerned was he to recreate nature itself in his poems — a bird singing, nesting or flying — rather than to evoke a human response to it that he was, in many ways, a forerunner of the contemporary poets whose poems comprise the bulk of this book.

The poems included have been chosen for their accuracy of detail and authenticity and because, in most cases, the poet's primary intention is to present birds as they are, rather than to use them as symbols to point some moral about life or human behaviour. It is true that, in a few, other considerations are introduced. For example, in 'Redwings', Patrick Dickinson draws a comparison between bird and poet and Leslie Norris touches on a similar idea at the end of 'Nightingales'; from winter gulls Alan Ross has a sense of insecurity and the transitory nature of the material world.

Then there are a few poems which can be read at two levels, such as R. S. Thomas' 'A Blackbird Singing' and 'Hawk Roosting' by Ted Hughes. However, a possible symbolic interpretation need not preclude an enjoyment of the poem on a literal level, for the birds are real and alive. Whether or not 'Hawk Roosting' is seen as a political allegory or a straightforward account of a hawk perched high in a tree, the poem is a powerful evocation of the cold-eyed hauteur of a bird of prey. In fact, the treatments of the subject are as many and varied as the different species of birds. Thrushes for Ted Hughes are terrible and terrifying, cold, coiled machines for killing; for John Clare they are 'Nature's minstrels ... glad as that sunshine and the laughing sky'.

There are also narrative poems, which convincingly recreate memorable personal experiences. Patrick Dickinson's first encounter with redwings is powerfully rendered, as are Leslie Norris' accounts of childhood experiences in 'Barn Owl' and 'Nightingales'. In the latter, the reader can feel the excitement and share the anticipation: 'Would it sing, would it sing?'

There is comedy, too. Norman MacCaig's 'Sparrow' is an example of wit in the Elizabethan sense, a happy metaphysical conceit, in which the proletarian bird, though lacking the culture, refinement and sophistication of some other species, passes the examination of life with flying colours. While the blackbird indulges himself writing 'pretty scrolls on the air with the gold nib of his beak', the sparrow prefers 'a punch-up in a gutter'. The humour is heightened by the combination of bathos and the vernacular. There is also the humour, in

'Wild Oats', of the beautiful female pigeon who causes such a stir — 'Mae West in the Women's Guild'. She is studiously ignored by the other females who continue dowdily with 'whatever pigeons do when they're knitting'.

Yet the humour is never at the expense of the birds involved. The portrayal is affectionate and, because it is based upon close observation, also apt. Richard Kell scrutinises the sheen on the neck feathers of pigeons:

> Elusive ghosts of sunshine
> Slither down the green gloss
> Of their necks an instant, and are gone.

The sounds, too, comic and familiar, are beautifully described:

> Only warm dark dimples of sound
> Slide like slow bubbles
> From the contented throats.

Precision and keen observation are features of so many of the poems selected. Norman MacCaig, for example, who appears more often than any other poet in this anthology, might reasonably be described as the John Clare of the twentieth century. For MacCaig the natural world is a continual source of wonder and his poetry shows the understanding he has for, and the joy he derives from, wild animals and birds. As with Clare, his poems often reveal a keen eye for detail. The darts and spurts of ringed plovers are beautifully suggested by the use of short vowel sounds, monosyllabic words and a staccato rhythm:

> They sprint eight feet and –
> Stop. Like that. They
> sprintayard (like that) and
> stop.
> They have no acceleration
> and no brakes.
> Top speed's their only one.

Just as no one who has ever searched for a nightingale's nest can doubt that John Clare was writing from experience, so nobody who has ever watched a heron will doubt that Norman MacCaig has keenly studied that spectral bird:

> It stands in water, wrapped in heron. It makes
> An absolute exclusion of everything else
> By disappearing in itself, yet is the presence
> Of hidden pools and secret, reedy lakes.

Time and time again, the poet marvels at the birds which he attempts to portray. John Heath-Stubbs describes how, as dusk approaches, starlings gather in their thousands at winter roosts:

> wheeling,
> Streaming and twisting, the whole murmuration
> Turning like one bird:

In 'The House Martins II', Michael Hamburger's swallows dive from the shed where they are nesting:

> Through a square gap in the panes
> Less wide than their wingspan.

and return with:

> a headlong dive
> Into familiar darkness.

And he seems to be expressing his sense of the inadequacy of language to capture completely the extravagance and breadth of bird life when he writes 'The smallest words are not small enough'.

Yet for a supreme example of what the poet can achieve, how close he can come to the actuality, we must turn to Ted Hughes' 'Swifts'.

Arriving from their winter quarters in late April or early May,

> The swifts
> Materialise at the tip of a long scream
> Of needle.

There is their marvellous flight:

> With a bowing
> Power-thrust to left, then to right, then a flicker they
> Tilt into a slide, a tremble for balance,
> Then a lashing down disappearance
> Behind elms.

The performance of the poet is as breathtaking as the flight of the swifts, the language as airborne and controlled, at once light and powerful: the movement of the verse *is* the flight of the birds:

> Frog-gapers,
> Speedway goggles, international mobsters ...
> They crowd their evening dirt-track meetings,
> Racing their discords, screaming as if speed-burned,
> Head-height, clipping the doorway
> With their leaden velocity and their butterfly lightness,
> Their too much power, their arrow-thwack into the eaves.

There is extraordinary compression of both language and ideas in this description, as there is in the account of the young swift incapable of effective flight. What a contrast between the bird's grotesque efforts on the ground,

> He bat-crawled on his tiny useless feet, tangling his flails
> Like a broken toy,

and his one and only brief and almost glorious flight:

> then suddenly he flowed away under
> His bowed shoulders of enormous swimming power,
> Slid away along levels wobbling
> On the fine wire they have reduced life to.

So perfectly matched are expression and subject that, when the flight fails and the bird crashes among the raspberries, the language crashes too.

There is truly stunning writing in this poem with its accuracy and graphic detail, extraordinary economy, suppleness and variety: the colloquial language of comic-strips ('thwack') and contemporary side-glances ('their evening dirt-track meeting') rest easily alongside the poignancy and classical allusion of the concluding lines:

> The inevitable balsa death.
> Finally burial
> For the husk
> Of my little Apollo –
>
> The charred scream
> Folded in its huge power.

Ted Hughes' language, too, is folded in its huge power. What the poet has created is almost as glorious as the swifts themselves. Almost.

This poem is considered at length here to underline the points made earlier about nature poets before John Clare and perhaps to convince those sceptics who cannot shake off a secret yearning for odes to nightingales and skylarks. The work of Hughes, MacCaig, Phoebe Hesketh and others proves without question the truth of Clare's contention that one day poems which presented nature, rather than used it, would 'be considered as great beautys'. The work of these contemporary poets would surely give Clare great pleasure, for in their poems the birds truly *exist*.

In the poems that follow, the reader is shown nature 'in close-up', through the eye of poet and painter. Andrew Young's poem, 'Field Glasses', is placed, quite deliberately, at the end of the selection to serve as an appropriate epilogue. For the poems that precede it are *our* field glasses and Young's words apply not just to the close observation of birds but to the enjoyment of the poems and paintings in this book:

> 'And while I stand and look,
> Their private lives in open book,
> I feel so privileged ...'

Mike Mockler 1982

———— PART ONE ————

Close to Home

BIRDS OF TOWN AND GARDEN

The brawling house sparrow, the rough-neck starling, the portly pigeon: familiar to us all but hardly the stuff of poetry. And yet why not? After all, they are much more a part of our lives than those stock birds of romantic poetry, the skylark, turtle dove and nightingale. If the poet holds the mirror up to nature anywhere around our homes today, the reflections will always include such birds as sparrow, starling, pigeon, robin, blackbird, thrush and wren. The eye of poet and artist notices what we miss and permits us to see and hear what we would otherwise overlook or take for granted. A starling singing in spring, for example:

> …blithering away
> Discords, with clichés picked up
> From the other melodists.

Or the movements of pigeons:

> as they stump about
> Their heads like tiny hammers
> Tap at imaginary nails
> In non-existent walls.

Town, or feral, pigeons have learned to live and breed in the busiest city centre so that they have become a part of city life. We walk amongst them, barely giving them a second glance and they display as little interest in us as they waddle from beneath our very feet. The house sparrow is the great pragmatist, the realist; he is no scholar but has graduated from the university of life and thrives when other birds perish:

> He carries what learning he has
> lightly – it is, in fact, based only
> on the usefulness whose result
> is survival.

Mundane birds they may be but they are among the most successful in the bird world; the survivors, which have struck up a long-lasting relationship with man and have adapted themselves to the world that he has created.

In 'The Robin', written when the poet was only sixteen, John Clare, in his concern for the welfare of the birds near his home in the depths of winter, is a forerunner of so many people today who try to help the local birds in the winter months. The kinship we feel with birds is also suggested by Norman Nicholson in 'The Cock's Nest'. The male wren builds several nests in his territory in spring and, having attracted a female by his singing, shows her his nests, one of which she will choose for the laying of the eggs. The other nests are ignored. For Nicholson the empty nest he finds matches the sense of loss and emptiness he feels at the death of his father.

The amazing achievement of migratory birds such as house martins which return year after year to nest under our eaves, having flown thousands of miles from Africa 'over glaciers, over high waves', is the subject of Michael Hamburger's two poems. That they arrive each year, without fail, 'in whatever wind', is a marvel to him and to us. When he writes 'Here they are. Again. Still' the single-word sentences underscore his incredulity, his inability to grasp the magnitude of their attainments. It is barely thinkable that, one day, they may not return.

The huge significance of the recurring appearance of these birds, whose presence it is easy to take for granted, is stressed by Ted Hughes when, with relief, he notes that the swifts have returned:

> They've made it again,
> Which means the globe's still working…

13

—— SPARROW ——

He's no artist.
His taste in clothes is more
dowdy than gaudy.
And his nest – that blackbird, writing
pretty scrolls on the air with the gold nib of his beak,
would call it a slum.

To stalk solitary on lawns,
to sing solitary in midnight trees,
to glide solitary over gray Atlantics –
not for him: he'd rather
a punch-up in a gutter.

He carries what learning he has
lightly – it is, in fact, based only
on the usefulness whose result
is survival. A proletarian bird.
No scholar.

But when winter soft-shoes in
and these other birds –
ballet dancers, musicians, architects –
die in the snow
and freeze to branches,
watch him happily flying
on the O-levels and A-levels
of the air.

Norman MacCaig

— ROBIN —

With a bonfire throat,
Legs of twig,
A dark brown coat,
The inspector robin
Comes where I dig.

Military man
With a bright eye
And a wooden leg,
He must scrounge and beg
Now the summer's by:

Beg at the doors,
Scrounge in the gardens,
While daylight lessens
And the grass glistens
And the ground hardens.

The toads have their vaults,
The squirrels their money,
The swifts their journey;
For him the earth's anger,
The taste of hunger.

And his unfrightened song
For the impending snows
Is also for the rose
And for the great Armada
And the Phoenician trader
And the last missile raider –
It's the only one he knows.

Hal Summers

— THE ROBIN —

Now the snow hides the ground, little birds leave the wood,
And fly to the cottage to beg for their food;
While the robin, domestic, more tame than the rest,
With its wings drooping down, and rough feathers undrest,
Comes close to our windows, as much as to say,
'I would venture in, if I could find a way:
I'm starv'd, and I want to get out of the cold;
Oh! make me a passage, and think me not bold.'
Ah, poor little creature! thy visits reveal
Complaints such as these to the heart that can feel;
Nor shall such complainings be urged in vain;
I'll make thee a hole, if I take out a pane.
Come in, and a welcome reception thou'lt find;
I keep no grimalkin to murder inclin'd.
But oh, little robin! be careful to shun
That house, where the peasant makes use of a gun;
For if thou but taste of the seed he has strew'd,
Thy life as a ransom must pay for the food:
His aim is unerring, his heart is as hard,
And thy race, though so harmless, he'll never regard.
Distinction with him, boy, is nothing at all;
Both the wren, and the robin, with sparrows must fall.
For his soul (though he outwardly looks like a man)
Is in nature a wolf of the Apennine clan;
Like them his whole study is bent on his prey:
Then be careful, and shun what is meant to betray.
Come, come to my cottage, and thou shalt be free
To perch on my finger and sit on my knee:
Thou shalt eat of the crumbles of bread to thy fill,
And have leisure to clean both thy feathers and bill.
Then come, little robin! and never believe
Such warm invitations are meant to deceive:
In duty I'm bound to show mercy on thee,
Since God don't deny it to sinners like me.

John Clare
(Written, in 1809,
at the age of 16)

— THE THRUSH'S NEST —

Within a thick and spreading hawthorn bush,
That overhung a molehill large and round,
I heard from morn to morn a merry thrush
Sing hymns to sunrise, and I drank the sound
With joy; and, often an intruding guest,
I watched her secret toils from day to day, –
How true she warped the moss to form a nest,
And modelled it within with wood and clay;
And by and by, like heath-bells gilt with dew,
There lay her shining eggs, as bright as flowers,
Ink-spotted-over, shells of greeny blue;
And there I witnessed, in the sunny hours,
A brood of Nature's minstrels chirp and fly,
Glad as that sunshine and the laughing sky.

John Clare

— THRUSHES —

Terrifying are the attent sleek thrushes on the lawn,
More coiled steel than living – a poised
Dark deadly eye, those delicate legs
Triggered to stirrings beyond sense – with a start, a bounce, a stab
Overtake the instant and drag out some writhing thing.
No indolent procrastinations and no yawning stares.
No sighs or head-scratchings. Nothing but bounce and stab
And a ravening second.

Is it their single-minded-sized skulls, or a trained
Body, or genius, or a nestful of brats
Gives their days this bullet and automatic
Purpose? Mozart's brain had it, and the shark's mouth
That hungers down the blood-smell even to a leak of its own
Side and devouring of itself: efficiency which
Strikes too streamlined for any doubt to pluck at it
Or obstruction deflect.

With a man it is otherwise. Heroisms on horseback,
Outstripping his desk-diary at a broad desk,
Carving at a tiny ivory ornament
For years: his act worships itself – while for him,
Though he bends to be blent in the prayer, how loud and above what
Furious spaces of fire do the distracting devils
Orgy and hosannah, under what wilderness
Of black silent waters weep.

Ted Hughes

— THE COCK'S NEST —

The spring my father died – it was winter, really,
February fill-grave, but March was in
By the time we felt the bruise of it and knew
How empty the rooms were – that spring
A wren flew to our yard, over Walter Willson's
Warehouse roof and the girls' school playground
From the old allotments that are now no more than a compost
For raising dockens and cats. It found a niche
Tucked behind the pipe of the bathroom outflow,
Caged in a wickerwork of creeper; then
Began to build:
Three times a minute, hour after hour,
Backward and forward to the backyard wall,
Nipping off neb-fulls of the soot-spored moss
Rooted between the bricks. In a few days
The nest was finished. They say the cock
Leases an option of sites and leaves the hen
To choose which nest she will. She didn't choose our yard.
And as March gambolled out, the fat King-Alfred sun
Blared down too early from its tinny trumpet
On new-dug potato-beds, the still bare creeper,
The cock's nest with never an egg in,
And my father dead.

Norman Nicholson

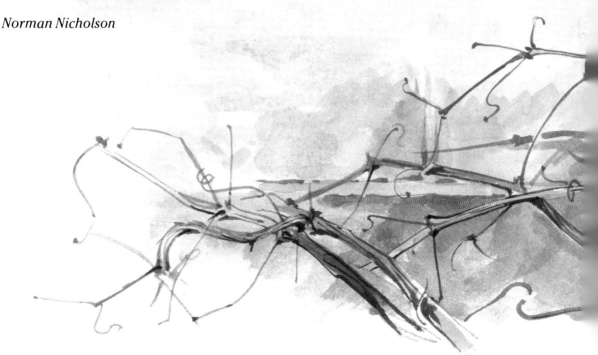

— THE HOUSE MARTINS —

Pines I remember, the air crisp.
Here, in a haze, elms I see,
Do not see, and hills hiding the river.

But the roof is generous,
Can preserve nests. And again the martins mutter
Their small-talk, daily domestic twitter
After those miles, deadly to some,
Over glaciers, over high waves.

Arrived, arrived in whatever wind,
To ride all winds and, housed on the windy side
Warm with their own blood, the cold mud walls.

Michael Hamburger

John
Tennent

— THE HOUSE MARTINS II —

I

Fifteen years later. From under an older roof.
In weather blown in from the north,
With roses that rot in bud, sodden.
In a colder, windier county:
Again that muttering, on the windy side of the house.

Fluttering exits, a jerkier tacking
Than the swallows' that, flashier, shoot
Into flight from their perches indoors,
On the sheltered side,
Through a square gap in the panes
Less wide than their wingspan.
Or the swallows' homing, a headlong dive
Into familiar darkness.

Never loud as the swifts that shriek as they swoop and glide
High up in great circles, and mate on the wing.

II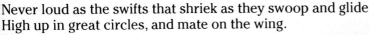

Again that muttering. A muted gabble,
Low gurgle under the eaves.

The smallest words are not small enough
To record them, the martins, and their small recurrence,
Their small defiance, of more and more.

So I repeat: fifteen years later.
Here they are. Again. Still.
And can perpetrate no infinities, for comfort,
Nor mouth the metaphors that will damn my kind
The summer I see their empty nests.

Michael Hamburger

— WILD OATS —

Every day I see from my window
pigeons, up on a roof ledge – the males
are wobbling gyroscopes of lust.

Last week a stranger joined them, a snowwhite
pouting fantail,
Mae West in the Women's Guild.
What becks, what croo-croos, what
demented pirouetting, what a lack
of moustaches to stroke.

The females – no need to be one of them
to know
exactly what they were thinking – pretended
she wasn't there
and went dowdily on with whatever
pigeons do when they're knitting.

Norman MacCaig

— PIGEONS —

They paddle with staccato feet
In powder-pools of sunlight,
Small blue busybodies
Strutting like fat gentlemen
With hands clasped
Under their swallowtail coats;
And, as they stump about,
Their heads like tiny hammers
Tap at imaginary nails
In non-existent walls.
Elusive ghosts of sunshine
Slither down the green gloss
Of their necks an instant, and are gone.

Summer hangs drugged from sky to earth
In limpid fathoms of silence:
Only warm dark dimples of sound
Slide like slow bubbles
From the contented throats.

Raise a casual hand –
With one quick gust
They fountain into air.

Richard Kell

— SWIFTS —

Fifteenth of May. Cherry blossom. The swifts
Materialise at the tip of a long scream
Of needle. "Look! They're back! Look!" And they're gone
On a steep

Controlled scream of skid
Round the house-end and away under the cherries. Gone.
Suddenly flickering in sky summit, three or four together,
Gnat-whisp frail, and hover-searching, and listening

For air-chills – are they too early? With a bowing
Power-thrust to left, then to right, then a flicker they
Tilt into a slide, a tremble for balance,
Then a lashing down disappearance

Behind elms.
                        They've made it again,
Which means the globe's still working, the Creation's
Still waking refreshed, our summer's
Still all to come –
                      And here they are, here they are again
Erupting across yard stones
Shrapnel-scatter terror. Frog-gapers,
Speedway goggles, international mobsters –

A bolas of three or four wire screams
Jockeying across each other
On their switchback wheel of death.
They swat past, hard-fletched,

Veer on the hard air, toss up over the roof,
And are gone again. Their mole-dark labouring,
Their lunatic limber scramming frenzy
And their whirling blades

Sparkle out into blue –
                          Not ours any more.
Rats ransacked their nests so now they shun us.
Round luckier houses now
They crowd their evening dirt-track meetings,

Racing their discords, screaming as if speed-burned,
Head-height, clipping the doorway
With their leaden velocity and their butterfly lightness,
Their too much power, their arrow-thwack into the eaves.

Every year a first-fling, nearly-flying
Misfit flopped in our yard,
Groggily somersaulting to get airborne.
He bat-crawled on his tiny useless feet, tangling his flails

Like a broken toy, and shrieking thinly
Till I tossed him up – then suddenly he flowed away under
His bowed shoulders of enormous swimming power,
Slid away along levels wobbling

On the fine wire they have reduced life to,
And crashed among the raspberries.
Then followed fiery hospital hours
In a kitchen. The moustached goblin savage

Nested in a scarf. The bright blank
Blind, like an angel, to my meat-crumbs and flies.
Then eyelids resting. Wasted clingers curled.
The inevitable balsa death.

                          Finally burial
For the husk
Of my little Apollo –

The charred scream
Folded in its huge power.

Ted Hughes

— SWIFTS —

The swifts winnow the air.
It is pleasant at the end of the day
To watch them. I have shut the mind
On fools. The phone's frenzy
Is over. There is only the swifts'
Restlessness in the sky
And their shrill squealing.

           Sometimes they glide,
Or rip the silk of the wind
In passing. Unseen ribbons
Are trailing upon the air.
There is no solving the problem
They pose, that had millions of years
Behind it, when the first thinker
Looked at them.

           Sometimes they meet
In the high air; what is engendered
At contact? I am learning to bring
Only my wonder to the contemplation
Of the geometry of their dark wings.

R. S. Thomas

— STARLINGS —

Can you keep it so,
cool tree, making a blue cage
for an obstreperous population? –
for a congregation of mediaeval scholars
quarrelling in several languages? –
for busybodies marketing
in the bazaar of green leaves? –
for clockwork fossils that can't be still even
when the Spring runs down?

No tree, no blue cage can contain
that restlessness. They whirr off
and sow themselves in a scattered handful
on the grass – and are
bustling monks
tilling their green precincts.

Norman MacCaig

— THE STARLING —

The starling is my darling, although
I don't much approve of its
Habits. Proletarian bird,
Nesting in holes and corners, making a mess,
And sometimes dropping its eggs
Just any old where – on the front lawn, for instance.

It thinks it can sing too. In springtime
They are on every rooftop, or high bough,
Or telegraph pole, blithering away
Discords, with clichés picked up
From the other melodists.

But go to Trafalgar Square,
And stand, about sundown, on the steps of St. Martin's;
Mark then in the air,
The starlings, before they roost, at their evolutions –
Scores of starlings, wheeling,
Streaming and twisting, the whole murmuration
Turning like one bird: an image
Realized, of the City.

John Heath-Stubbs

John Tennent

— A Blackbird Singing —

It seems wrong that out of this bird,
Black, bold, a suggestion of dark
Places about it, there yet should come
Such rich music, as though the notes'
Ore were changed to a rare metal
At one touch of that bright bill.

You have heard it often, alone at your desk
In a green April, your mind drawn
Away from its work by sweet disturbance
Of the mild evening outside your room.

A slow singer, but loading each phrase
With history's overtones, love, joy
And grief learned by his dark tribe
In other orchards and passed on
Instinctively as they are now,
But fresh always with new tears.

R. S. Thomas

— ROOKERY —

Here they come, freckling the sunset,
The slow big sailers bearing down
On the plantation. They have flown
Their sorties and are now well met.

The upper twigs dip and wobble
With each almost two-point landing,
Then ride to rest. There is nothing
Else to do now only settle.

But they keep up a guttural chat
As stragglers knock the roost see-saw.
Something's satisfied in that caw.
Who wouldn't come to rest like that?

Seamus Heaney

— SOLITARY CROW —

Why solitary crow? He in his feathers
Is a whole world of crow – of a dry-stick nest,
Of windy distances where to be crow is best,
Of tough-guy clowning and of black things done
To a sprawled lamb whose blood beads in the sun.

Sardonic anarchist. Where he goes he carries,
Since there's no centre, what a centre is,
And that is crow, the ragged self that's his.
Smudged on a cloud, he jeers at the world then halts
To jeer at himself and turns two somersaults.

He ambles through the air, flops down and seesaws
On a blunt fencepost, hiccups and says Caw.
The sun glints greasy on his working craw
And adds a silver spot to that round eye
Whose black light bends and cocks the world awry.

Norman MacCaig

— WINTER GULLS —

Treetops, spires and houses – all have grown
Plumper under overcoats of snow: a rubber-coloured morning
Where square-gardens are knee-deep in silence. Everything
Is muffled but solid: a district of respectable footsteps.
Now the albino sun lights in some crows
That claw stiffly at branches with talons like forceps.

Suddenly, to patches of slate visible like baldness
Under snow, a scurry of gulls comes wheeling white
Past the window. The snow where they vainly grip
Flurries into air, a waste-paper world that slips.
What was reassuring before now seems aimless and light,
And the whole skyline unreliable, skittish as a kite.

Soon it recovers, and a hypocrite air descends
That tries to persuade us that life is just as before.
But now we know different – for the gulls,
Startled, gave us the tip that nothing
In quite the same way will be ever secure –
For us, fated to drift on a glitter that dulls;
Like them, effigies stuffed on painted and scented hulls.

Alan Ross

— THE REDWING —

The winter clenched its fist
And knuckles numb with frost
Struck blind at the blinding snow.
It was hard for domestic creatures,
Cows, humans, and such, to get
Shelter and warmth and food.
And then the redwings came,
Birds of the open field,
The wood, the wild, only
Extremity makes them yield.

I must admit that never
Before that day when thaw
Bled red to white in the west
Had I seen a redwing, but there
Where ivy-berries offered
A last everlasting lost
Hope of life I held
A redwing in my hand,
Still warm, and was it dead?
It had toppled from a tree
Too weak too frail to fill
Its crop before the frost
Again asked for the cost
Of a winter dosshouse rest.
So I saw what it was like.

Never before had I seen
A redwing, now a hundred
Hopped through the shivering town
Unrecognised, unknown
To most who saw them save
Simply as 'birds'. They came
As poets come among us,
Driven in from the wild
Not asking nor expecting
To be recognised for what
They are – if they are not
The usual thrush you can
Identify them dead.

I held it in my hand,
I knew that it was dead,
But still I willed it to live
Not asking nor expecting
Many to understand
Why I must will it so.
But I know what a redwing is,
And I know how I know.

Patrick Dickinson

— BARN OWL —

Ernie Morgan found him, a small
Fur mitten inexplicably upright,
And hissing like a treble kettle
Beneath the tree he'd fallen from.
His bright eye frightened Ernie,
Who popped a rusty bucket over him
And ran for us. We kept him
In a backyard shed, perched
On the rung of a broken deck-chair,
Its canvas faded to his down's biscuit.
Men from the pits, their own childhood
Spent waste in the crippling earth,
Held him gently, brought him mice
From the wealth of our riddled tenements,
Saw that we understood his tenderness,
His tiny body under its puffed quilt,
Then left us alone. We called him Snowy.

He was never clumsy. He flew
From the first like a skilled moth,
Sifting the air with feathers,
Floating it softly to the place he wanted.
At dusk he'd stir, preen, stand
At the window-ledge, fly. It was
A catching of the heart to see him go.
Six months we kept him, saw him
Grow beautiful in a way each thought
His own knowledge. One afternoon, home
With pretended illness, I watched him
Leave. It was daylight. He lifted slowly
Over the Hughes's roof, his cream face calm,
And never came back. I saw this;
And tell it for the first time,
Having wanted to keep his mystery.

And would not say it now, but that
This morning, walking in Slindon woods
Before the sun, I found a barn owl
Dead in the rusty bracken.
He was not clumsy in his death,
His wings folded decently to him,
His plumes, unruffled orange,
Bore flawlessly their delicate patterning.
With a stick I turned him, not
Wishing to touch his feathery stiffness.
There was neither blood nor wound on him,
But for the savaged foot a scavenger
Had ripped. I saw the sinews.
I could have skewered them out
Like a common fowl's. Moving away
I was oppressed by him, thinking
Confusedly that down the generations
Of air this death was Snowy's
Emblematic messenger, that I should know
The meaning of it, the dead barn owl.

Leslie Norris

— Blackbird —

My wife saw it first –
I was reading the evening paper.
Come and look, she said.

It was trying to drink
Where water had formed on a drain-cover.
It was shabby with dying.
It did not move until I was very close –
Then hopped off, heavily,
Disturbing dead leaves.

We left water, crumbs.
It did not touch them
But waited among the leaves,
Silently.

This morning was beautiful:
Sunlight, other birds
Singing.

It was outside the door.
I picked it up
And it was like holding feathered air.
I wrapped what was left
Incongruously
In green sycamore leaves
And buried it near the tree,
Inches down.

This evening
I find it difficult to concentrate
On the paper, the news
Of another cosmonaut.

Christopher Leach

— DEAD BLACKBIRD —

The blackbird used to come each day
listening, head sideways, for movement under the lawn,
stabbing his yellow-as-crocus bill
precisely in,
pulling out a pink elastic worm.

In winter with flirted tail
he landed on the sill for crumbs
ousting sparrows, blue-tits – even robins.
Soot-black, sleek,
his plumage shone like a dark man's head.

But this morning I looked out of the window
and saw him dead –
a crumpled bunch of feathers
rocking in the wind.

I have never seen anything dead
except flies
and stuffed animals in museums
where they make them look alive.
Dead people are hidden away,
tidied into boxes,
covered with flowers.
The living talk about the dead in low voices.
Is death so ugly, uncomfortable
that people are afraid?

I am much more afraid of what I cannot see.
But I can see the blackbird;
and know these crumpled feathers
are only rags of him, not he
with his crocus-yellow bill.

Phoebe Hesketh

— MAN AND BEAST —

Hugging the ground by the lilac tree,
With shadows in conspiracy,

The black cat from the house next door
Waits with death in each bared claw

For the tender unwary bird
That all the summer I have heard

In the orchard singing. I hate
The cat that is its savage fate,

And choose a stone with which to send
Slayer, not victim, to its end.

I look to where the black cat lies,
But drop my stone, seeing its eyes –

Who is it sins now, those eyes say,
You the hunter, or I the prey?

Clifford Dyment

PART TWO

The Wide Open Spaces

There are some birds whose natures seem to match the cold, grey wastes, windswept shorelines and the bleak hilltops of the far north. They are seen at their best in such settings and, when they travel to less remote places, they carry with them the aura of those desolate haunts. Even their calls hold the suggestion of mist-shrouded wilderness. Curlew and greenshank, for example, may be encountered in sheltered estuaries and bays, sometimes even on flooded water meadows on farmland, but no one who has heard their mournful and plaintive calls can doubt that the wild hills and windblown moors where they breed are their true spiritual homes.

Norman MacCaig knows these places and knows the birds that haunt them. His poems capture the birds in their settings and the totality of the experience. As he watches, in a spacious Scottish seascape, a group of gannets fishing — a staggeringly spectacular sight as they drop, head-first like javelins, from terrifying heights — he recreates the entire scene so vividly that the reader feels that he is there with him sharing the experience. As well as the diving gannets, MacCaig notices a seal 'struggling in the waistcoat of its own skin', and points out to the reader where the wind 'has moulded the sand in pastry frills'.

So vast and breathtaking are the landscapes, so wild and elusive the birds which are a part of them, that they pose a major problem for the poet. MacCaig touches on the dilemma when he writes of the greenshank's call:

> His single note – one can't help calling it
> piping, one can't help
> calling it plaintive . . .

For the poet must revitalise language, lift out words that glint and sparkle, that are clean and fresh enough to capture the whole texture of nature. What words but 'plaintive' to use of a greenshank's call, or 'desolate' of the cry of the curlew? What else but 'arrogant' or 'fierce' of the bird of prey? Language must be stretched taut, pulled this way and that, if the poet is to evoke the richness and colour of the natural world. He must attempt to express the inexpressible:

> Space opens and from the heart of the matter
> sheds a descending grace that makes,
> for a moment, that naked thing, being,
> a thing to understand.

— RHU MOR —

Gannets fall like the heads of tridents,
bombarding the green silk water
off Rhu Mor. A salt seabeast of a timber
pushes its long snout
up on the sand, where a seal,
struggling in the straitwaistcoat of its own skin,
violently shuffles towards the frayed wave,
the spinning sandgrains, the
caves of green.

I sit in the dunes – the wind
has moulded the sand in pastry frills
and cornices: flights of grass
are stuck in it – their smooth shafts shiver
with trickling drops of light.

Space opens and from the heart of the matter
sheds a descending grace that makes,
for a moment, that naked thing, being,
a thing to understand.

I look out from it
at the grave and simple elements
gathered round a barrage of gannets
whose detonations
explode the green into white.

Norman MacCaig

— GREENSHANK —

His single note – one can't help calling it
piping, one can't help
calling it plaintive – slides droopingly down
no more than a semitone, but is filled
with an octave of loneliness, with the whole sad scale
of desolation.

He won't leave us. He keeps flying
fifty yards and perching
on a rock or a small hummock,
drawing attention to himself.
Then he calls and calls
and flies on again
in a flight
roundshouldered but dashing,
skulking yet bold.

Cuckoo, phoenix, nightingale,
you are no truer emblems
than this bird is.
He is the melancholy that flies
in the weathers of my mind,
He is the loneliness that calls to me there
in a semitone
of desolate octaves.

Norman MacCaig

— CURLEW —

Dropped from the air at evening, this desolate call
Mocks us, who listen to its delicate non-humanity.
Dogs smile, cats flatter, cows regard us all
With eyes like those of ladies in a city,

So that we transfer to them familiar human virtues
To comfort and keep us safe. But this adamant bird
With the plaintive throat and curved, uneasy jaws
Crying creates a desert with a word

More terrible than chaos, and we stand at the edge
Of nothing. How shall we know its purpose, this wild bird,
Whose world is not confined by the linnets' hedge,
Whose mouth lets fly the appalling cry we heard?

Leslie Norris

— Chough —

Desolate that cry as though world were unworthy.
See now, rounding the headland, a forlorn hopeless bird,
trembling black wings fingering the blowy air,
dainty and ghostly, careless of the scattering salt.

This is the cave-dweller that flies like a butterfly,
buffeted by daws, almost extinct, who has chosen,
so gentle a bird, to live on furious coasts.

Here where sea whistles in funnels, and slaps the backs
of burly granite slabs and hisses over holes,
in bellowing hollows that shelter the female seal
the Cornish chough wavers over the waves.

By lion rocks, rocks like the heads of queens,
sailing with ragged plumes upturned, into the wind
goes delicate indifferent the doomed bird.

Rex Warner

John Tennent

SOMETHING TOLD THE WILD GEESE

Something told the wild geese
 It was time to go.
Though the fields lay golden
 Something whispered, 'Snow.'

Leaves were green and stirring,
 Berries, lustre-glossed,
But beneath warm feathers
 Something cautioned, 'Frost.'

All the sagging orchards
 Steamed with amber spice,
But each wild breast stiffened
 At remembered ice.

Something told the wild geese
 It was time to fly –
Summer sun was on their wings,
 Winter in their cry.

Rachel Field.

ARTHUR GEE

— THE FLIGHT OF THE GEESE —

I hear the low wind wash the softening snow,
　　The low tide loiter down the shore. The night
　　Full filled with April forecast, hath no light.
The salt wave on the sedge-flat pulses slow.
Through the hid furrows lisp in murmurous flow
　　The thaw's shy ministers; and hark! The height
　　Of heaven grows weird and loud with unseen flight
Of strong hosts prophesying as they go!
High through the drenched and hollow night their wings
　　Beat northward hard on winter's trail. The sound
Of their confused and solemn voices, borne
Athwart the dark to their long Arctic morn,
　　Comes with a sanction and an awe profound,
A boding of unknown, foreshadowed things.

Charles G. D. Roberts

—LAPWING—

Leaves, summer's coinage spent, golden are all together whirled,
sent spinning, dipping, slipping, shuffled by heavy handed wind,
shifted sideways, sifted, lifted, and in swarms made to fly,
spent sunflies, gorgeous tatters, airdrift, pinions of trees.

Pennons of the autumn wind, flying the same loose flag,
minions of the rush of air, companions of draggled cloud,
tattered, scattered pell mell, diving, with side-slip suddenly wailing
as they scale the uneasy sky flapping the lapwing fly.

Plover, with under the tail pine-red, dead leafwealth in down displayed,
crested with glancing crests, sheeny with seagreen, mirror of movement
of the deep sea horses plunging, restless, fretted by the whip of wind
tugging green tons, wet waste, lugging a mass to Labrador.

See them fall wailing over high hill tops with hue and cry,
like uneasy ghosts slipping in the dishevelled air,
with ever so much of forlorn ocean and wastes of wind
in their elbowing of the air and in their lamentable call.

Rex Warner

PART THREE

Under Cover of Darkness

Bird of ill-omen, in league with the forces of evil, a dark and sinister presence in folklore and legend for hundreds of years: this is the popular view of the owl. Yet, surely, this conflicts with the other image of a kindly, wise old man in children's story-books, rotund and cuddly with a friendly, humanoid face.

How can the two images be resolved? Neither is accurate yet both contain elements of truth: owls suggest both and it is easy to see how two such contradictory ideas grew up. When at rest, eyeing one inscrutably through half-closed eyes, calmly and deliberately turning its head, an owl can appear more human than bird, more fluffy toy than killer. When hunting with silent, slow wing-beats, dropping to seize a victim in large hooked talons, tearing flesh from the bone, the owl is a beautiful yet deadly predator.

It is this side which Glyn Hughes captures so admirably in his poem, 'Owls', as he describes the barn owl hunting over snow-covered fields, on 'moth-muffled wings'. The whole scene is presented with almost photographic sharpness, details keenly observed and accurately portrayed. Even so, the legendary idea forces its way in near the end:

> they say that someone dies
> in the house over which he cries.

So too, Laurie Lee, writing of the tawny owl, feels compelled to introduce the idea of darker forces:

> I shudder in my private chair.
> For like an augur he has come.

Of course, there is nothing ominous about the hoots and shrieks of an owl: they are merely part of the social life of the bird, the calls and song being its communication signals, no more sinister than the songs and calls of robin, blackbird or thrush.

— Owls —

Two cinders of the fiery sunset
cooled in a tree-hole or stone-crevice sleep

awoke with moth-muffled wings to hook
the landscape in their flight.

In winter they flowed on white fields. The shrieking silence
of the dark things in darkness was more magnetic than light

a silence made luminous. One wingtwist made a glow
of the white breast of one on the ridge as he watched the other;

the wall was white from which they leapt
across field and canal to pin a mouse
and with no time for shock or shriek
a titbit was ferried to the one who watched at the nest.

Once I roused one from his daytime half-sleep.
As he blundered drunken through the light

small birds skidded from him, gathered, and mobbed.
Strange dweller between day and night:

they say that someone dies
in the house over which he cries.

Glyn Hughes

— GREY OWL —

When fireflies begin to wink
over the stubble near the wood,
ghost-of-the-air,
the grey owl, glides into dusk

Over the spruce, a drift of smoke,
over the juniper knoll,
whispering wings
making the sound of silk unfurling,
in the soft blur of starlight
a puff of feathers blown about.

Terrible fixed eyes,
talons sheathed in down,
refute this floating wraith.

Before the shapes of mist
show white beneath the moon,
the rabbit or the rat
will know the knives of fire,
the pothooks swinging out of space.

But now the muffled hunter
moves like smoke, like wind,
scarcely apprehended,
barely glimpsed and gone,
like a grey thought
fanning the margins of the mind.

Joseph Payne Brennan

— TOWN OWL —

On eves of cold, when slow coal fires,
rooted in basements, burn and branch,
brushing with smoke the city air;

When quartered moons pale in the sky,
and neons glow along the dark
like deadly nightshade on a briar;

Above the muffled traffic then
I hear the owl, and at his note
I shudder in my private chair.

For like an augur he has come
to roost among our crumbling walls,
his blooded talons sheathed in fur.

Some secret lure of time it seems
has called him from his country wastes
to hunt a newer wasteland here.

And where the candelabra swung
bright with the dancers' thousand eyes,
now his black, hooded pupils stare,

And where the silk-shoed lovers ran
with dust of diamonds in their hair,
he opens now his silent wing,

And, like a stroke of doom, drops down,
and swoops across the empty hall,
and plucks a quick mouse off the stair . . .

Laurie Lee

— THE FERN-OWL'S NEST —

The weary woodman, rocking home beneath
His tightly banded faggot, wonders oft,
While crossing over the furze-crowded heath,
To hear the fern-owl's cry, that whews aloft
In circling whirls, and often by his head
Whizzes as quick as thought and ill at rest,
As through the rustling ling with heavy tread
He goes, nor heeds he tramples near its nest,
That underneath the furze or squatting thorn
Lies hidden on the ground; and teasing round
That lonely spot, she wakes her jarring noise
To the unheeding waste, till mottled morn
Fills the red east with daylight's coming sound
And the heath's echoes mock the herding boys.

John Clare

PART FOUR

Where Peaceful Waters Flow

Few birds can claim to be more popular than mallards, whose charm attracts adults and children with bags of breadcrumbs to river, pond and lake. Their comic gaucheness on land and familiar quackings and cluckings are as much a part of their attraction as their grace and beauty in the water or their gloriously fast and direct flight. These contrasting elements are beautifully caught by the first three poems in this section.

F. W. Harvey finds that ducks offer solace from the troubles of the world: they were created

> . . . in case the minds of men
> Should stiffen and become
> Dull, humourless and glum.

However, Phoebe Hesketh, watching a mother with her ducklings 'nuzzling joyful mud', realises, when a stoat attacks, that the world of nature is not cute, homely and peaceful. Similarly, Rex Warner reminds us that most ducks are not tame but wild, migratory birds as perfectly at home in the air as on water:

> with wings like garden-shears clipping the misty air,
> four mallard, hard-winged, with necks like rods
> fly in perfect formation over the marsh.

For many, the bird-life of a river, lake or shore extends little further than ducks and swans which wait to be fed and show no fear of humans. Other, shyer birds are less readily seen. The ringed plover, a bird of mud-flat and shingle, blends perfectly with the gravel until its sudden, sharp, darting movements catch one's eye. And it is on stony beaches where the tern colonies are to be found. Terns are summer visitors, light-winged and buoyant in flight, stunning and spectacular in their sudden dives. Their colonies are raucous and crowded places, scenes of continual movement, especially when a human intruder causes the entire adult population to fountain upwards as in Patrick Dickinson's poem, 'Common Terns'.

The heron, one of the largest and most stately of waterside birds, is by contrast, usually a silent bird, the very epitome of patient stealth. It will stand quite motionless in the shallows, hunched and neckless, like a grotesque stone sculpture. On a grey winter's day, the heron becomes part of the misty stillness.

Not so the kingfisher, which seems a refugee from some tropical land. For this bird, words like 'flash', 'sparkle' and 'jewel' are inadequate. Just as words fall short of the kingfisher's brilliant colours, so the eye can barely take in the full beauty of the bird as it flashes away from view. Then, as so often with birds, it is later that the glory of the event is fully enjoyed. The bird may have gone

> Yet bright as a bead behind the eye,
> The image blazes on.

— DUCKS —

I

From troubles of the world
I turn to ducks,
Beautiful comical things
Sleeping or curled
Their heads beneath white wings
By water cool,
Or finding curious things
To eat in various mucks
Beneath the pool,
Tails uppermost, or waddling
Sailor-like on the shores
Of ponds, or paddling
– Left! right! – with fanlike feet
Which are for steady oars
When they (white galleys) float
Each bird a boat
Rippling at will the sweet
Wide waterway . . .
When night is fallen *you* creep
Upstairs, but drakes and dillies
Nest with pale water-stars,
Moonbeams and shadow bars
And water-lilies:
Fearful too much to sleep
Since they've no locks
To click against the teeth
Of weasel and fox.
And warm beneath
Are eggs of cloudy green
When hungry rats and lean
Would stealthily suck
New life, but for the mien,
The bold ferocious mien,
Of the mother-duck.

II

Yes, ducks are valiant things
On nests of twigs and straws,
And ducks are soothy things
And lovely on the lake
When that the sunlight draws
Thereon their pictures dim
In colours cool.

And when beneath the pool
They dabble, and when they swim
And make their rippling rings,
O ducks are beautiful things!

But ducks are comical things:
As comical as you.
Quack!
They waddle round, they do.
They eat all sorts of things.
And then they quack.
By barn and stable and stack
They wander at their will,
But if you go too near
They look at you through black
Small topaz-tinted eyes.
And wish you ill.
Triangular and clear
They leave their curious track
In mud at the water's edge,
And there amid the sedge
And slime they gobble and peer
Saying 'Quack! quack!'

III

When God had finished the stars and whirl of coloured suns
He turned His mind from big things to fashion little ones,
Beautiful tiny things (like daisies) He made, and then
He made the comical ones in case the minds of men
   Should stiffen and become
   Dull, humourless and glum:
And so forgetful of their Maker be
As to take even themselves – *quite seriously.*
Caterpillars and cats are lively and excellent puns:
All God's jokes are good – even the practical ones!
And as for the duck, I think God must have smiled a bit
Seeing those eyes blink on the day He fashioned it.
And he's probably laughing still at the sound that came
   out of its bill!

F. W. Harvey

— MALLARD —

Squawking they rise from reeds into the sun,
climbing like furies, running on blood and bone,
with wings like garden-shears clipping the misty air,
four mallard, hard-winged, with necks like rods
fly in perfect formation over the marsh.

Keeping their distance, gyring, not letting slip the air,
but leaping into it straight like hounds or divers,
they stretch out into the wind and sound their horns again.

Suddenly siding to a bank of air unbidden
by hand signal or morse message of command
downsky they plane, sliding like corks on a current,
designed so deftly that all air is advantage,

till with few flaps, orderly as they left earth,
alighting among curlew they pad on mud.

Rex Warner

— THE MALLARD —

Brown-checked, neat as new spring tweed,
A mallard, wing-stretched in the sun,
Watched from the bank of a beer-bubble stream
Her ducklings, one after one,
Daring, dipping in dazzling weed,
Nuzzling joyful mud.
Black and yellow, downy as bees,
They busied about a fringe of reed
In a paddled nursery pool.

The mother, content, lay dry,
Relaxed her wings, slackened her throat,
Dared to close one bead-black eye
When swift as terror a lightning stoat
Forked and flashed upstream.

Spatter and splash of mother and young –
Feathered drops whirled in a storm of fear,
Water thrashed in flight.
A stone for the stoat – I flung it near
And stood alone, not knowing what fate
Lay crouched in wait, while the stillness there
Grew ominous and bright.

Phoebe Hesketh

—RINGED PLOVER BY A WATER'S EDGE —

They sprint eight feet and –
stop. Like that. They
sprintayard (like that) and
stop.
They have no acceleration
and no brakes.
Top speed's their only one.

They're alive – put life
through a burning-glass, they're
its focus – but they share
the world of delicate clockwork.

In spasmodic
Indian file
they parallel the parallel ripples.

When they stop
they, suddenly, are
gravel.

Norman MacCaig

— THE HERON —

On lonely river-mud a heron alone
Of all things moving – water, reeds, and mist –
Maintains his sculptured attitude of stone.
A dead leaf floats on the sliding river, kissed
By its own reflection in a brief farewell.
Movement without sound; the evening drifts
On autumn tides of colour, light, and smell
Of warm decay; and now the heron lifts
Enormous wings in elegy; a grey
Shadow that seems to bear the light away.

Phoebe Hesketh

— Heron —

It stands in water, wrapped in heron. It makes
An absolute exclusion of everything else
By disappearing in itself, yet is the presence
Of hidden pools and secret, reedy lakes.
It twirls small fish from the bright water flakes.

(Glog goes the small fish down.) With lifted head
And no shoulders at all, it periscopes round –
Steps, like an aunty, forward – gives itself shoulders
And vanishes, a shilling in a pound,
Making no sight as other things make no sound.

Until, releasing its own spring, it fills
The air with heron, finds its height and goes,
A spear between two clouds. A cliff receives it
And it is gargoyle. All around it hills
Stand in the sea; wind from a brown sail spills.

Norman MacCaig

KINGFISHER

Brown as nettle-beer, the stream
Shadow-freckled, specked with sun,
Slides between the trees.

Not a ripple breaks in foam;
Only the frilled hedge-parsley falls
White upon the ground.
No insect drills the air; no sound
Rustles among the reeds.
Bird and leaf and thought are still
When shot from the blue, a kingfisher
Flashes between the ferns –
Jewelled torpedo sparkling by
Under the bridge and gone –
Yet bright as a bead behind the eye,
The image blazes on.

Phoebe Hesketh

— COMMON TERNS —

Quiet as conscience on the Stock Exchange
I crept across a gradient of shelving shingle
To where in a gravel-working water lay
Brackish and thick with weed, slate-blue and viscous.

Out on a spit were common terns in hundreds:
Terns with their delicate staggered swallow-wings
And striding lilting flight and hovering flutter
Like kestrels into the wind, and sheer stoop
Straight for the darting goby in the pool.

And as I rose above the shingle crest
They burst into the air like an explosion,
A white gusher, a quarter-mile-high fountain
Mushrooming out into fragments, yet each perfect,
A column of shrieking milling sound-at-pressure,
Terribly like man's work – as if they were
An atomic bomb and I some engineer.

I felt my human agony then to the full,
That I for simile of that natural vision
Should so conclusively immediately choose
Utter destruction absolute desolation;
And sat there numb and grievous, ashamed to move,
As wildly they whirled and wheeled and slowly settled,
Bright sediment down the blue glass of air.

Patrick Dickinson

PART FIVE

'Killers from the Egg'

BIRDS OF PREY

The birds of prey have an indefinable yet irresistible appeal. No other members of the bird world can quite match their magnificent flight, whether soaring effortlessly on outspread wings or stooping after their quarry with breathtaking speed. The hooked beak, fierce talons, and cold, glinting eye combine to create an impression of arrogant majesty.

For the hawk in Ted Hughes' 'Hawk Roosting', there is nothing in life but 'the allotment of death': even in sleep, the bird rehearses perfect kills. The verse — a series of bald, emphatic statements — perfectly matches the bird's character. The arrogance is such that the hawk considers all of creation, the high branches of the trees, the air's buoyancy and the earth below, to have been formed for him alone. To anyone who has watched a bird of prey floating overhead or perched motionless on high, this all sounds chillingly real. And the grim reality of the kill is graphically highlighted in A. C. Benson's poem: the hawk has fed, the small song bird is no more, and over the heather drifts 'the down from a bleeding breast'.

Nature is indeed 'red in tooth and claw' but the bird of prey is 'not without pity for he does not know pity'; though a machine for killing, he 'kills without cruelty for he does not know cruelty'. Would that this were so of man who has no such excuse. For, although Nature has equipped these birds supremely well for survival in the natural world, she reckoned without man. Callously slaughtered by gamekeepers so that the huntsman can have his sport, senselessly persecuted by selfish and greedy egg-collectors and falconers and threatened more terribly by man's poisonous chemicals, the birds of prey are precariously positioned at the top of a food chain, the links of which are being corroded away.

Leslie Norris gives us a buzzard who is master of the air:

With infinitely confident little variations of his finger-ends
He soothes the erratic winds.
He hangs on air's gap, then turns
On royal wing into his untouchable circle.

The quintessential bird of prey — untamable, untouchable, invincible. It is pleasant to think so but sadly today this is a romantic illusion. In his poem, Richard Church presents a hawk as a sombre threat, imminent and terrible. But how much more terrible and sombre is the threat posed by man.

— THE HAWK —

The hawk slipt out of the pine, and rose in the sunlit air:
Steady and still he poised; his shadow slept on the grass:
And the bird's song sickened and sank; she cowered with furtive
 stare
Dumb, till the quivering dimness should flicker and shift and
 pass.

Suddenly down he dropped: she heard the hiss of his wing,
Fled with a scream of terror: oh, would she had dared to rest!
For the hawk at eve was full, and there was no bird to sing,
And over the heather drifted the down from a bleeding breast.

A. C. Benson

— THE HAWK —

The hawk! He stands on air,
  Treads it down, height over height.
He fixes with his dreadful stare
  One earthbound, furry mite.

Solitary in the sky
  He leans on either wing,
And closes with that cruel eye
  Ten acres in a ring.

Above that sunken realm he rides
  And swoops whene'er he will
On leveret, mouse, and all besides,
  Far chosen for his kill.

The lesser birds unite in fear
  And flutter to attack.
He veers aside as they draw near,
  Hangs poised, and then swerves back.

Alone once more, with pinions spread
  He now resumes his stare
For prey already doomed and dead,
  Though it is unaware.

Fate with talons, fate with wings,
  Fate with unerring eye,
Shadowing all terrestrial things –
  The pinpoint in the sky!

Richard Church

— Hawk —

Things motionless were felt to move
Downwards: the hedges crawled
Down steep sun-molten banks to where
The shrunken river sprawled:

Dark cloud-ravines of shadow flowed
Sheer down the dark wood's cliff;
Draped heavily in golden heat,
The limbs of air felt stiff:

And, threatening doom, the sky's concentrated will
Hung in one black speck, poised above the hill.

George Rostrevor Hamilton

— Buzzard —

With infinitely confident little variations of his finger-ends
He soothes the erratic winds.
He hangs on air's gap, then turns
On royal wing into his untouchable circle.

All, all, lie under his sifting eye,
The squat man, the sheep, the mouse in the slate cleft.

He is not without pity for he does not know pity.
He is a machine for killing; searchlight eye,
Immaculate wing, then talon and hook.
He kills without cruelty for he does not know cruelty.

If he fails in a small death he is awkward. And angry,
Loosing upon the hills his terrible, petulant cry.
To fail often is to die.
His livelihood is such single-minded and obsessional artistry.

He is not seduced by emotion
Or impeccable clear thought even
Into considerations other than his pure life.

We observe our prey doubtfully,
Behind many hedges and in tufted country.
Even when we see it clear
Have too many words to kill it.

Leslie Norris

Simon Turvey

— THE EAGLE —

He clasps the crag with hookéd hands;
Close to the sun in lonely lands,
Ringed with the azure world, he stands.

The wrinkled sea beneath him crawls;
He watches from his mountain walls,
And like a thunderbolt he falls.

Lord Tennyson

— THE EAGLE —

He hangs between his wings outspread
   Level and still
And bends a narrow golden head,
   Scanning the ground to kill.

Yet as he sails and smoothly swings
   Round the hill-side,
He looks as though from his own wings
   He hung down crucified.

Andrew Young

— Marsh Harrier —

Female: Hickling Broad, 3 September 1980

Over the reed horizons, far left,
Dark feather fingered,
Enter Death, sweeping low.
She wears a golden helmet
   radiant,
And a mask from which
Her dark eyes peer.
Her minions the mobbing
   lapwings,
Give warning of her royal
   hunt,
Vituperating those who lag.
She is not contemptuous of
   their attentions . . .
Nor of those who tarry
To pay their homage.

Peter Partington

— HAWK ROOSTING —

I sit in the top of the wood, my eyes closed.
Inaction, no falsifying dream
Between my hooked head and hooked feet:
Or in sleep rehearse perfect kills and eat.

The convenience of the high trees!
The air's buoyancy and the sun's ray
Are of advantage to me;
And the earth's face upward for my inspection.

My feet are locked upon the rough bark.
It took the whole of Creation
To produce my foot, my each feather:
Now I hold Creation in my foot

Or fly up, and revolve it all slowly –
I kill where I please because it is all mine.
There is no sophistry in my body:
My manners are tearing off heads –

The allotment of death.
For the one path of my flight is direct
Through the bones of the living.
No arguments assert my right:

The sun is behind me.
Nothing has changed since I began.
My eye has permitted no change.
I am going to keep things like this.

Ted Hughes

PART SIX

In Woodland and Field

To enter a wood is to enter the most rich and complex of wildlife habitats. Every twig and branch, every leaf and trunk supports a life form of some kind. The casual walker should not be deceived by the stillness and silence into thinking that the wood is devoid of life. In a brief visit, few of the sixty or more species of bird which regularly inhabit woodland will be seen; most will slip away out of sight as soon as the human intruder appears. Only with extreme patience and understanding, such as John Clare displays in his search for the nightingale's nest, will the visitor gain anything more than a very superficial impression of woodland birds.

If he sits still and waits for long enough he will see the life of the wood return to normal. The blackcap will resume singing, confirming Clare's opinion that it is 'a nightingale in melody'. A pheasant may tip-toe gingerly by, 'sure as an Inca priest', or a party of long-tailed tits may flit past, tut-tutting, oblivious of the human presence. Their tiny, busy activity is so accurately portrayed by Rex Warner:

All the spinney is active with churr and bat-squeak,
with flutter, flit, dip, dropping buoyant of bodies through the air,
jostling of cones, twig springing, twirling to ground of needles . . .

The watcher must remain still and suffer minor discomforts like mosquitoes that 'dart and nip', if he is to be rewarded with unforgettable sights such as a woodpecker feeding its young at its nest-hole in a tree, 'leaning back from her trunk like an abseiler'. Or he may be fortunate to see a cock redstart, surely the most colourful of woodland birds. In a sun-dappled wood, as the redstart moves from tree to tree with its constantly quivering orange tail, it is as if the bird is carrying around its own personal pool of sunlight.

The onlooker can only admire and feel grateful for what he has seen. At such times, the blackcaps, nightingales, woodpeckers and redstarts 'can make up for everything'.

103

— LONGTAILED TIT —

All the spinney is active with churr and bat-squeak,
with flutter, flit, dip, dropping buoyant of bodies through the air,
jostling of cones, twig springing, twirling to ground of needles,
as tits and goldcrests swing and hustle in the bunchy trees.

Busy the goldcrest, high squeaking, under the needly
green fall of leaf forgetting the North Sea,
in inches of light whole-hearted, a spot of spirit.

The longtail lunging and lingering through the air,
a mouse, rush-tail, a ball, wool-feather, peeper,
looking so sharp through cherry blankets of down,
the doll-face easy on the flying twig's trapeze,
pink and white in the light, as light as blowing seed,
is meek in merriment, all careless of air's bitterness,
the bare-tooth coming, bark-biting of the winter wind.

Rex Warner

— AFTER THE WOODPECKER —

Mosquitoes dart and nip
Everywhere; rhododendrons
Suck and smother the soil;
    the earth is hard,
    the eyehole small,
But the woodpecker can make up for everything.

She knew we were there:
Shirt bright in sunlight
Made her cock her head,
    rattle her grub-filled
    throat and wait,
Leaning back from her trunk like an abseiler;

The classic pose, beak
Poised, not to peck
But to plunge to where
    her young clustered,
    hungry and clicking
Like clocks just assembled and not quite the ticket.

I shall let them all know,
In wash-basin banter,
Through dinner-plate clatter,
    or briskly down corridors
    past close-shut rooms:
The woodpecker can make up for everything.

D. W. Ashbee

— THE NIGHTINGALE'S NEST —

Up this green woodland-ride let's softly rove,
And list the nightingale – she dwells just here.
Hush! let the wood-gate softly clap, for fear
The noise might drive her from her home of love;
For here I've heard her many a merry year –
At morn, at eve, nay, all the livelong day,
As though she lived on song. This very spot,
Just where that old man's beard all wildly trails
Rude arbours o'er the road and stops the way –
And where that child its bluebell flowers hath got,
Laughing and creeping through the mossy rails –
There have I hunted like a very boy,
Creeping on hands and knees through matted thorn
To find her nest and see her feed her young.
And vainly did I many hours employ:
All seemed as hidden as a thought unborn.
And where those crimping fern-leaves ramp among
The hazel's under-boughs, I've nestled down
And watched her while she sung; and her renown
Hath made me marvel that so famed a bird
Should have no better dress than russet brown.
Her wings would tremble in her ecstasy,
And feathers stand on end, as 'twere with joy,
And mouth wide open to release her heart
Of its out-sobbing songs. The happiest part
Of summer's fame she shared, for so to me
Did happy fancies shapen her employ;
But if I touched a bush or scarcely stirred,
All in a moment stopt. I watched in vain:
The timid bird had left the hazel bush,
And at a distance hid to sing again.
Lost in a wilderness of listening leaves,
Rich ecstasy would pour its luscious strain,
Till envy spurred the emulating thrush
To start less wild and scarce interior songs;
For while of half the year care him bereaves,
To damp the ardour of his speckled breast,
The nightingale to summer's life belongs,
And naked trees and winter's nipping wrongs
Are strangers to her music and her rest.
Her joys are evergreen, her world is wide –
Hark! there she is as usual – let's be hush –
For in this blackthorn-clump, if rightly guessed,
Her curious house is hidden. Part aside
These hazel branches in a gentle way
And stoop right cautious 'neath the rustling boughs,
For we will have another search to-day

And hunt this fern-strewn thorn-clump round and round;
And where this reeded wood-grass idly bows,
We'll wade right through, it is a likely nook:
In such like spots and often on the ground,
They'll build, where rude boys never think to look.
Ay, as I live! her secret nest is here,
Upon this whitethorn stump! I've searched about
For hours in vain. There! put that bramble by –
Nay, trample on its branches and get near.
How subtle is the bird! she started out,
And raised a plaintive note of danger nigh,
Ere we were past the brambles; and now, near
Her nest, she sudden stops – as choking fear
That might betray her home. So even now
We'll leave it as we found it: safety's guard
Of pathless solitudes shall keep it still.
See there! she's sitting on the old oak bough,
Mute in her fears; our presence doth retard
Her joys, and doubt turns every rapture chill.
Sing on, sweet bird! may no worse hap befall
Thy visions than the fear that now deceives.
We will not plunder music of its dower,
Nor turn this spot of happiness to thrall;
For melody seems hid in every flower
That blossoms near thy home. These harebells all
Seem bowing with the beautiful in song;
And gaping cuckoo, with its spotted leaves,
Seems blushing with the singing it has heard.
How curious is the nest! no other bird
Uses such loose materials, or weaves
Its dwelling in such spots: dead oaken leaves
Are placed without and velvet moss within,
And little scraps of grass, and – scant and spare,
Of what seem scarce materials – down and hair;
For from men's haunts she nothing seems to win.
Yet nature is the builder, and contrives
Homes for her children's comfort even here,
Where solitude's disciples spend their lives
Unseen, save when a wanderer passes near
Who loves such pleasant places. Deep adown
The nest is made, a hermit's mossy cell.
Snug lie her curious eggs in number five,
Of deadened green, or rather olive-brown;
And the old prickly thorn-bush guards them well.
So here we'll leave them, still unknown to wrong,
As the old woodland's legacy of song.

John Clare

— NIGHTINGALES —

I

My namesake, old Bill Norris, standing beneath a tree
So bitterly gnarled he might have grown from it, stopped
Talking to listen, lifted eyes dayblue and delighted,
And laughed a silent pleasure. 'There's a good many,'
He said, 'Walks past as close as you and never hears her,
Though she sings as bright in the hot noon as any night.'
Two feet above his head the dun bird pulsed and lilted.
It was in this village and perhaps for this same bird
I lay awake the whole of one miraculous darkness.
She sang so close to my house I could have touched
Her singing; I could not breathe through the aching silences.
And for nights after, hunched among pillows, I grabbed
At any sleep at all, hearing the nightingale
Hammer my plaintive rest with remorseless melody.
Full of resented ecstasy, I groaned nightlong in my bed.

II

Or driving one Sunday morning in Maytime Hampshire
On our way to a christening in one of the villages,
We stopped on Steep Hill, the road climbing headily upwards.
In the first warm air of the year we looked down on the
Trees, unmoving and full in the freshness of their leaves.
There were eight nightingales, eight, they filled the valley
With sobbing, the cataracts of their voices fell
Erratically among the splendid beeches. Open-eyed
We stood on the lip of the hill, while near and far
The water-notes of their singing grew faint, were lost almost,
Answered and redoubled near at hand, trailed
Dropping sadly down the valley-sides, struck purely out
With sound round notes into the listening morning
We were still with music, as the day was. That we were late
For the christening was to the credit of those nightingales.

III

When I was very young my father took me from bed,
Dressed me in haste, and we walked into the night.
Winter was so long gone I had forgotten darkness.
We went by paths which in daylight knew me well,
But now were strange with shadow. It was not long
Before we came to the wood where the nightingale sang,
The unbelievable bird who lived in the stories
Of almost my every book. Would it sing, would it sing?
I thought the wood was full of silent listeners.
I do not remember it singing. My father carried me home,
My head rolling back on its stalk at every measure
Of his deep stride, and all I have brought back
From that long night are the fixed stars reeling.
It is the poet's bird, they say. Perhaps I took it home,
For here I am, raising my voice, scraping my throat raw again.

Leslie Norris

— PHEASANT —

Cock stubble-searching pheasant, delicate
Stepper, Cathayan bird, you fire
The landscape, as across the hollow lyre
Quick fingers burn the moment: call your mate
From the deep woods tonight, for your surprised
Metallic summons answers me like wire
Thrilling with messages, and I cannot wait
To catch its evening import, half-surmised.
Others may speak these things, but you alone
Fear never noise, make the damp thickets ring
With your assertions, set the afternoon
Alight with coloured pride. Your image glows
At autumn's centre – bright, unquestioning
Exotic bird, haunter of autumn hedgerows.

Sidney Keyes

— COCK-PHEASANT —

Gilded with leaf-thick paint; a steady
Eye fixed like a ruby rock;
Across the cidrous banks of autumn
Swaggers the stamping pheasant-cock.

The thrusting nut and bursting apple
Accompany his jointed walk,
The creviced pumpkin and the marrow
Bend to his path on melting stalk.

Sure as an Inca priest or devil,
Feathers stroking down the corn,
He blinks the lively dust of daylight,
Blind to the hunter's powder-horn.

For me, alike, this flushed October –
Ripe, and round-fleshed, and bellyful –
Fevers me fast but cannot fright, though
Each dropped leaf shows the winter's skull.

Laurie Lee

— THE BLACKCAP —

The blackcap is a singing bird,
 A nightingale in melody;
Last March in Open Wood I heard
 One sing that quite astonished me;
I took it for the nightingale –
 It jug-jugged just the same as he –
So creeping through the mossy rail
 I in the thicket got to see:

When one small bird of saddened green,
 Black head, and breast of ashy grey,
In ivied oak tree scarcely seen,
 Stopt all at once and flew away;
And since, in hedgerow's dotterel trees,
 I've oft this tiny minstrel met,
Where ivy flapping to the breeze
 Bear ring-marked berries black as jet;
But whether they find food in these
 I've never seen or known as yet.

John Clare

R.Millington

— REDSTART IN A WELSH WOOD —

Lichen drips green light
Under trees that grapple together;
Moss muffles dark knuckles of cragside.
Young ferns are wafted by currents
In the underwater gloom
Where grey cobwebs float from bark.

Then suddenly you are there,
Glowing with the sun of Africa,
Trailing behind you shimmering fires.
Nervous and trembling
You sprinkle the glades with flickering light,
Your tail aflame in its own heat-haze;
As you drop to the ground
It touches Welsh grindstone
And sparks fly.
Then up again on a quivering branch
To powder the leaves with fiery dust.
Where you are it is sunlight.

But now the sunlight is gone.
Bare trees tie hillsides
In tight knots.
Lichen weeps black tears
And the wood waits for the Redstart's return.

Mike Mockler

PART SEVEN
An Infinite Variety

So, after all, what is the attraction of wild birds; wherein lies their charm? Is it simply that they are unattainable and free? In 'The Ecstatic', C. Day Lewis expresses the breathless wonder we feel, our sense of their elusiveness. Is it the apparently limitless range of behaviour, their very movements which are part of the large fabric of nature, as we see in Norman MacCaig's poem, 'Movements'? What is it that fires the imagination of poet and painter, intrigues the scientist and satisfies the common man?

There is no single answer, of course. Every bird, every wing-beat, every song-note, every feather is an answer in itself. Faced with such an infinite variety, we can only humbly stand and watch and, like Andrew Young in the final poem, feel grateful for the privilege.

— THE ECSTATIC —

Lark, skylark, spilling your rubbed and round
Pebbles of sound in air's still lake,
Whose widening circles fill the noon; yet none
Is known so small beside the sun:

Be strong your fervent soaring, your skyward air!
Tremble there, a nerve of song!
Float up there where voice and wing are one,
A singing star, a note of light!

Buoyed, embayed in heaven's noon-wide reaches –
For soon light's tide will turn – Oh stay!
Cease not till day streams to the west, then down
That estuary drop down to peace.

C. Day Lewis

— MOVEMENTS —

Lark drives invisible pitons in the air
And hauls itself up the face of space.
Mouse stops being comma and clockworks on the floor.
Cats spill from walls. Swans undulate through clouds.
Eel drills through darkness its malignant face.

Fox, smouldering through the heather bushes, bursts
A bomb of grouse. A speck of air grows thick
And is a hornet. When a gannet dives
It's a white anchor falling. And when it lands
Umbrella heron becomes walking-stick.

I think these movements and become them, here,
In this room's stillness, none of them about,
And relish them all – until I think of where,
Thrashed by a crook, the cursive adder writes
Quick V's and Q's in the dust and rubs them out.

Norman MacCaig

Demirvels

1st year.

Grey Heron — adult.

Adder — Heysioc
3.6.75

— FIELD-GLASSES —

Though buds still speak in hints
And frozen ground has set the flints
As fast as precious stones
And birds perch on the boughs, silent as cones,

Suddenly waked from sloth
Young trees put on a ten years' growth
And stones double their size,
Drawn nearer through field-glasses' greater eyes.

Why I borrow their sight
Is not to give birds a fright
Creeping up close by inches;
I make the trees come, bringing tits and finches.

I lift a field itself
As lightly as I might a shelf,
And the rooks do not rage
Caught for a moment in my crystal cage.

And while I stand and look,
Their private lives an open book,
I feel so privileged
My shoulders prick, as though they were half-fledged.

Andrew Young

Acknowledgements

THE POEMS

Every effort has been made to trace the copyright holders of the poems reproduced in this anthology and the anthologist and publisher would like to thank the following for their permission to use the poems listed below. They would be pleased to hear from the copyright holders of any other poems used herein.

D. W. Ashbee: 'After the Woodpecker' by D. W. Ashbee.

The Bodley Head: 'Long-tailed Tit'; 'Lapwing'; 'Mallard'; 'Chough' by Rex Warner from *Poems*.

Jonathan Cape Ltd, The Hogarth Press and the Executors of the Estate of C. Day Lewis: 'The Ecstatic' by C. Day Lewis from *Collected Poems*.

Chatto and Windus Ltd: 'Pigeons' by Richard Kell from *Differences;* 'The Redwing' by Patrick Dickinson from *The World I See;* 'Common Terns' by Patrick Dickinson from *The Sailing Race;* 'Barn Owl' by Leslie Norris from *Mountains, Polecats, Pheasants;* 'Nightingales'; 'Curlew'; 'Buzzard' by Leslie Norris from *Finding Gold;* 'Kingfisher'; 'Dead Blackbird' by Phoebe Hesketh from *A Song of Sunlight*.

Faber and Faber Ltd: 'Thrushes'; 'Hawk Roosting' by Ted Hughes from *Lupercal;* 'Swifts' by Ted Hughes from *Season Songs*.

Granada Publishing Ltd: 'Swifts' by R. S. Thomas from *Pièta;* 'A Blackbird Singing' by R. S. Thomas from *Selected Poems 1946-1968*.

Michael Hamburger: 'The House Martins I' from *Travelling;* 'The House Martins II'.

Seamus Heaney: 'Rookery' by Seamus Heaney.

William Heinemann Ltd: 'The Hawk' by Richard Church from *The Burning Bush;* 'Hawk' by G. R. Hamilton from *Unknown Lovers and other Poems*.

Phoebe Hesketh: 'The Heron'; 'The Mallard' by Phoebe Hesketh from *Prayer for the Sun*.

David Higham Associates Ltd: 'The Cock's Nest' by Norman Nicholson from *A Local Habitation* published by Faber and Faber.

The Hogarth Press Ltd: 'Sparrow'; 'Wild Oats'; 'Greenshank'; 'Rhu Mor'; 'Feeding Ducks'; 'Ringed Plovers by a Water's Edge'; 'Heron'; 'Movements' by Norman MacCaig from *Old Maps and New;* 'Starlings'; 'Solitary Crow' by Norman MacCaig from *Rings on a Tree*.

Laurie Lee: 'Cock Pheasant' by Laurie Lee.

MacMillan, London and Basingstoke: 'The Killing of Sparrows' by Patricia Beer from *The Estuary*.

McGraw-Hill Ryerson Ltd, Toronto: 'The Flight of the Geese' by Sir Charles G. D. Roberts from *The Collected Poems of Sir Charles G. D. Roberts*.

Martin, Secker and Warburg Ltd: 'Field-Glasses'; 'The Eagle' by Andrew Young from *Complete Poems* edited by Leonard Clark.

Oxford University Press: 'Robin' by Hal Summers from *Tomorrow is my Love* © Hal Summers 1978.

Routledge and Kegan Paul Ltd: 'Pheasant' by Sidney Keyes from *Collected Poems*.

Sidgwick and Jackson Ltd: 'Ducks' by F. W. Harvey from *Ducks and Other Poems*.

THE PAINTINGS

With the exception of the late Dr. Eric Ennion's painting of Ringed Plovers resting on the Dunes reproduced on page 118 by kind permission of The Marler Gallery, Ludlow, all the paintings in this book were executed especially to enhance the poems with which they are presented. They are the work of the following artists:

John Broadhurst: Swifts pp 28-29; A Blackbird Singing pp 34-35; Lapwing pp 62-63; Redstart in a Welsh Wood pp 116-117

David Capewell: The Nightingale's Nest pp 108-109

John Davis: The Thrushes Nest p 18, and Thrushes p 19; Rookery pp 36-37 and, detail, p 12; The Mallard pp 78-79; Nightingales pp 110-111 and, detail, p 102

Sarah de'Ath: Man and Beast pp 48-49

Melvyn Gates: Curlew pp 56-57; Ringed Plover by a Water's Edge pp 80-81

Arthur Gee: Something Told The Wild Geese p 60 and, detail, p 50; The Flight of the Geese p 61; The Fern Owl's Nest pp 70-71

Robert Greenhalf: Rhu Mor pp 52-53; The Eagle p 96; The Eagle p 97

Rob Hume: Common Terns pp 86-87

Josephine Martin/The Garden Studio: Sparrow pp 14-15; Wild Oats p 24; Pigeons p 25; Barn Owl pp 44-45; Ducks pp 74-75; Field Glasses pp 124-125

Richard Millington: The Blackcap pp 114-115

Peter Partington: Swifts pp 26-27 and pp 2-3; Starlings pp 30-31; Mallard pp 76-77; Marsh Harrier pp 98-99; Movements pp 122-123

Alastair Proud: Owls pp 66-67; The Hawk pp 90-91; Hawk Roosting pp 100-101, and, detail, p 88

John Reaney: The Hawk p 92; Hawk p 93; The Ecstatic pp 120-121

Jennie Schofield: The Redwing pp 42-43; Grey Owl p 68; Town Owl p 69, and, detail, p 64; Kingfisher pp 84-85, and, detail, p 72; The Pheasant p 112; Cock Pheasant p 113

Joan Selwood/The Garden Studio: The Cock's Nest pp 20-21; Long-tailed Tit pp 104-105

John Tennent: The House Martins I p 22; The House Martins II p 23; The Starling pp 32-33; Winter Gulls pp 40-41; Chough pp 58-59; The Heron p 82; Heron p 83

Simon Turvey: Solitary Crow pp 38-39; Greenshank pp 54-55; Buzzard pp 94-95

James Williamson-Bell: Robin p 16; The Robin p 17; Blackbird p 46; Dead Blackbird p 47; After the Woodpecker pp 106-107

Index of poems

Index of first lines